Gram & Gramps~

I love you so much you both are

such a special bless___ ___.

Thank you for all ___ ___ and

wisdom. Both of ___ ___ have taught

me what true love feels like

I love you.

Love,
Laura Lemieux

The Gift of Years

from

Joan + Ray

With all our love

October 1997.

This book is dedicated to the joy-filled memory of my father, who loved life, and lived love

Published by
Lion Publishing plc
Sandy Lane West, Oxford, England
ISBN 0 7459 3006 9
Albatross Books Pty Ltd
PO Box 320, Sutherland, NSW 2232,
Australia
ISBN 0 7324 1230 7

First edition 1982

A catalogue record for this book is
available from the British Library

Printed and bound in Singapore

Picture acknowledgments
Jon Arnold: Lengthening Shadows; Neil
Beer: The Oak, The Good Life, Peace in
the Pain, Landmark, All Your Care, Keep
Me Young, Comforted Beyond Measure,
Something Beautiful; Image Bank: (David
de Lossy) Dark Days, (Andy Cauldfield)
On the Other Side; Skjold Photography:
Life is for Living, Across the Years, First
Grandchild, A Wider Family, My Future
Self, True Greatness; Telegraph Colour
Library: (B. Losh) cover & What is a
Grandmother?; ZEFA: (Marc Vaughn)
The Gift of Years

Text acknowledgments
'The Good Life' from *The Time of Your
Life* by Herb and Mary Montgomery,
Winston Press; 'First Grandchild' from
Hold Me up a Little Longer, Lord by
Marjorie Holmes, copyright © 1977
Marjorie Holmes Mighell, reprinted by
permission of Hodder & Stoughton Ltd
and Doubleday and Company, Inc; 'Keep
Me Young' ('I have been giving thought')
from *You have a minute, Lord?* by David
Kossoff, reprinted by permission of
Robson Books Ltd.

The Gift of
Years

Written and compiled by
Marion Stroud

A LION BOOK

The Gift of Years

The gift of years is an invisible package that must be opened and enjoyed one day at a time. It is a gift that we can neither buy nor hoard, nor should we take it for granted for it is not presented to all in equal measure.

The gift of years contains freedom from old ties, but responsibility for new ones. It holds joy and pain, laughter and tears, change and growth.

Within its wrappings we discover the next-but-one generation with whom we must learn new ways of relating. We struggle to become those who are willing to receive as well as to share; to hold out our life-learned wisdom in an open hand, so that it can be accepted or rejected at will.

The gift of years may hold bodily weakness and limitations but it can also contain increased spiritual strength and effectiveness.

The gift of years must simply be received with thanksgiving for it is the gift of life itself.

The Oak

Live thy life
Young and old
Like yon oak,
Bright in Spring,
Living gold;

Summer – rich
Then; and then
Autumn – changed,
Soberer-hued,
Gold again.

All his leaves
Fall'n at length
Look, he stands
Trunk and bough
Naked strength.

ALFRED TENNYSON

The Good Life

Many of us spend time believing that the 'good life' is going to begin some time in the future. It's going to be great when we've got enough money, when we meet someone who truly understands us, when we have our own business, when we retire. But life doesn't begin in the future. Right now is the time of our life! When we realize this, the hours we have take on greater worth. We see clearly that using our time well is important because each minute is a miracle that cannot be repeated.

Making the most of every moment is no accident. Those who live life to the full do so with design and purpose. They realize the value of time and see the world as a place of wonder and new possibilities.

HERB AND MARY MONTGOMERY

If you want to do something, do it today. Say sorry, show someone you love them now. If you have had a row, make it up. Don't waste time.

DAPHNE HAMILTON FAIRLEY

The good life is a process, not a state of being. It is a direction, not a destination.

CARL ROGERS

Life is for Living

There is no experience from which you can't learn something. When you stop learning, you stop living in any vital and meaningful sense. And the purpose of life, after all, is to live it, to taste experience to the utmost, to reach out eagerly and without fear for newer and richer experience.

ELEANOR ROOSEVELT

Many times the only way we can find out what is possible is by finding out what is not possible – in other words, by making a mistake.

NELSON BOSWELL

The man who never made a mistake never made anything.

ANON

Peace in the Pain

We have been promised a safe arrival but not a smooth voyage.

HENRY DUBANVILLE

Before the winds that blow do cease,
Teach me to dwell within thy calm;
Before the pain has passed in peace,
Give me, my God, to sing a psalm;
Let me not lose the chance to prove
The fulness of enabling love.

AMY CARMICHAEL

We know that in all things God works for
the good of those who love him.

PAUL: FROM THE NEW TESTAMENT

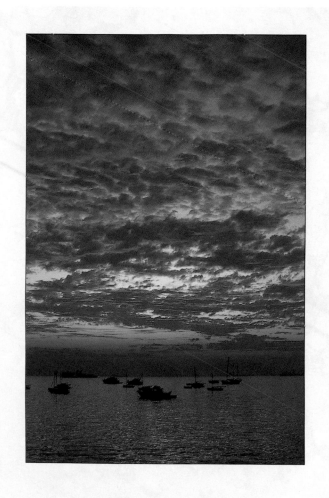

Dark Days

To protect them from pain. Surely this is what every mother longs to do. To shield them from the hurts, the problems and the pressures of life. To gather them up in my arms as once I could do, and soothe their tears with a kiss, a cuddle and a gentle word.

But life is not like that any more. Although I sometimes pray, 'Lord, let me take it for them – I can bear it, let them go free', I know this is not God's way. His loving dealings with us involve correction, testing and dark days, as well as laughter, joy and sunlit pathways. And the one without the other would produce a lopsided character, weak and underdeveloped in young and old alike.

So I cannot protect them from pain. I can only stand there with them in it – available but not intrusive, loving but not smothering, watchful but not inquisitive. And I can pray. Not for an easy journey, but for the stout shoes of faith and courage and love, which will enable them to tread the roughest path in safety.

Across the Years

Grandparents need grandchildren to keep the changing world alive for them. And grandchildren need grandparents to help them know who they are and to give them a sense of human experience in a world they cannot know.

MARGARET MEAD

A grandfather has the wisdom of long experience and the love of an understanding heart. He is more interested in the happiness of his children and grandchildren than anything else in the world. He can reminisce with them and share their dreams with interest and enthusiasm. He is the head of a family that loves him and looks up to him with respect and pride. He is a wonderful man to know and love.

DEAN WALLEY

First Grandchild

Thank you, God, that it's here, our first grandchild!

I hang up the telephone, rejoicing. I gaze out the window, dazzled and awed. 'Just a few moments ago,' he said. 'A beautiful little girl.'

She arrived with the sunrise, Lord. The heavens are pink with your glory. Radiance streams across the world.

The very trees lift up their branches as if in welcome, as if to receive her. And I want to fling out my arms, too, in joy and gratefulness and welcome.

My arms and my heart hold her up to you for blessing.

Oh, Lord, thank you for her and bless her, this little new life that is beginning its first day.

MARJORIE HOLMES

What is a Grandmother?

A grandmother is a lady who has no children of her own. She likes other people's little girls and boys.

Grandmothers don't have to do anything except to be there. They're old so they shouldn't play hard or run. It is enough if they take us to the market where the pretend horse is, and have a lot of pennies ready. Or if they take us for walks, they should slow down past things like pretty leaves and caterpillars. They should never say 'hurry-up'.

Usually grandmothers are fat, but not too fat to tie your shoes. They wear glasses and funny underwear. They can take their teeth and gums off.

Grandmothers don't have to be smart, only answer questions like, 'Why isn't God married?' and 'How come dogs chase cats?'

Grandmothers don't talk baby-talk like visitors do, because it is hard to understand. When they read to us, they don't skip or mind if it is the same story over again.

Everybody should try to have a grandmother, especially if you don't have television, because they are the only grown-ups who have time.

A NINE YEAR OLD

A Wider Family

I thought that I had come to terms with the pain, Lord. But it is back, washed in on a tidal wave of other people's family joy. Why did I have to meet them all today? Jenny – a grandmother by Christmas, she says; Margaret trying on that ridiculous hat for her son's wedding; and Christine, full of her visit to her daughter's family on the other side of the world. And while I smiled and congratulated them, my heart cried out all over again 'Why, God? Why have we been excluded from this beautiful and exclusive club called Parenthood?'

My husband feels it too Lord! Other men have the exploits of their children and grandchildren to enliven their conversation and brighten their lives. They may grumble about the expense and the anxiety, but they would never exchange their situation for his.

Please help me Lord. Deal with the hurt and that corroding self pity that sears my heart like a branding iron. And please reassure me – that there WILL be someone somewhere, who will welcome our visits when we are old.

I know that I need to focus on the good things that have enriched our life. Children of our own we may have lacked . . . but never love. Love of family . . . friends and most constant of all your love; a priceless gift which brightens the future and gently dispels the darkness of today – I thank you Lord.

Landmark

Birthdays are special days, Lord. Days on which to look back, to take stock and dream a little. And yet I wondered. Could this day really be a cause for celebration, marking the ending of her working life. How would she feel?

Of course I should have known, Lord. My fears were foolishness. There were no ifs or buts to mar her day. With laughter she accepted our good wishes, then spoke with joy of all that lies ahead.

'Today I reach the turning point of sixty! A landmark, certainly,' she said, 'but one I reach with great excitement. Don't pity me. For I would not change places with a single one of you. I would not choose to be either one day older or a moment younger. My heavenly Father planned that I should reach this age, at this time, while living in this place, for his good purpose. This day marks both an end and a beginning. The past I leave with him without regret and step out joyfully to meet the future he has planned.'

Every day and every hour is a new beginning with God. It makes no difference what the past has contained . . . the present and the future are all with which we need to be concerned.

DONALD GREY BARNHOUSE

My Future Self

*T*here was a time in my own life when I wondered about the value of
growing and being old. No more. I do not want to miss my old age any more
than I would choose to have skipped childhood or adolescence. But I do feel
an increased sense of responsibility to this future self, and to all those whose
lives may cross my path. What kind of old man will I be, given the chance?
The answer to that question depends largely on the kind of person I am right
now. For growing old is an ongoing project... through the lifespan.

ROBERT KASTENBAUM

You can't control the length of your life,
    but you can control its width and depth.
You can't control the contour of your countenance,
    but you can control its expression.
You can't control the other person's opportunities,
    but you can grasp your own...
Why worry about things you can't control?
Get busy controlling things that depend on you.

MYRON J. TAYLOR

True Greatness

**Try not to become a man of success,
but a man of value.**

It seemed as if the whole world came: civic officials and business colleagues; strangers too, who valued your work. They came to your memorial with kind words, taking the front seats, anxious to see and be seen.

But now, five long years on, who really remembers you? Not the well known, but ordinary people — those whose lives you touched with words of counsel, loving words of hope and faith. Those to whom you spoke of Jesus and challenged to commit their lives to him.

They are the living memorials; lasting tributes to a lifetime's investment which will survive into eternity. An investment which will receive the only accolade that really matters: 'Well done, good and faithful servant; enter into the joy of your Lord.'

Lengthening Shadows

I would say to those who mourn, look on each day that comes as a challenge, as a test of courage. The pain will come in waves, some days worse than others, for no apparent reason. Accept the pain. Little by little you will find new strength, new vision, born of the very pain and loneliness which seem, at first, impossible to master.

DAPHNE DU MAURIER

*From tomorrow on
I shall be sad.
From tomorrow on —
not today.
Today I will be glad,
and every day
no matter how bitter it may be
I shall say
From tomorrow on I shall be sad,
not today.*

JEWISH GIRL IN A CONCENTRATION CAMP

All Your Care

All of your care – tomorrow with its problems,
The lengthening shadows of the passing days,
The secret fears, of failure, weakness suffering,
Of grief and loss, and straightened lonely ways,
Leave it with Him, your future He will share,
For you are His, the object of His care.

JOAN SUISTED

The time comes to most of us when, whether we like it or not, old age and failing powers force us into solitude. Many people dread this time, and of course we cannot lapse into laziness and become an increasing burden to others. We must keep going while we can. But inevitably we shall become more and more alone.
If we have longed for solitude and learned to love it because we find God there, it should be that the last years of a long life will be the happiest of all, lived so close to Him, that His love and life can shine through us to countless souls.

MARGARET EVENING

Keep Me Young

I have been giving thought, Lord
— you have a minute? — to getting old.
Natural enough as the years pass . . .

So, Lord, please keep me young in the mind.
   Let me enjoy, Lord, let me enjoy.
If creaky I must be, and many-spectacled,
   and morning-stiff and food-careful,
If trembly-handed and slow-moving and
   breath-short and head-noddy,
I won't complain. Not a word.
If, with your help, dear Friend, there
   will dwell in this ancient monument,
A Young Mind. Please, Lord?

DAVID KOSSOFF

On the Other Side

Jesus said . . . 'I am the resurrection and the life.
He who believes in me will live, even though he
dies; and whoever lives and believes in me
will never die.'

JOHN'S GOSPEL

*Just as a good mariner, when he draws near to the harbour, lets down his
sails and enters it gently with slight headway on; so we ought to let down the
sails of our worldly pursuits and turn to God with all our heart, so that we
may come to that haven with all composure, and with all peace . . . There is,
in such a death, no pain nor any bitterness; but as a ripe apple lightly and
without violence detaches itself from its bough, so our soul severs itself from
the body where it has dwelt.*

DANTE ALIGHIERI

*'My sword I give to him who shall succeed me in my pilgrimage and my
courage and skill to him who can get it. My marks and scars I carry with me
as a sign that I have fought His battles who will now be my rewarder.' So Mr
Valiant for Truth passed over and all the trumpets sounded for him on the
other side.*

JOHN BUNYAN

Comforted Beyond Measure

There'll be no fear in heaven! 'He who sits on the throne will spread his tent over them.' That's a picture of heaven where all our fears will vanish in God's protecting presence.

There'll be no hunger or thirst. That's a picture of complete satisfaction which none of us can ever fully know on earth. But when we see Jesus face to face . . . there will be no inner cravings or emptiness.

There will be no suffering: 'The sun will not beat upon them, nor any scorching heat.' There will be no depressions, neuroses, anxieties, pressures, tensions, tiredness or old age.

There will be no loneliness: 'The Lamb at the centre of the throne will be their Shepherd; he will lead them to springs of living water.'

There will be no tears: 'God will wipe away every tear from their eyes.' Every cause of sadness will disappear in God's presence. We will be comforted beyond measure.

DAVID WATSON

Something Beautiful

'The Lord will perfect that which concerns me . . .'

THE BOOK OF PSALMS

'He who began a good work in you will carry it on to completion . . .'

PAUL: FROM THE NEW TESTAMENT

Something beautiful, something good,
All my confusion He understood.
All I had to offer Him
Was brokenness and strife,
But He made something beautiful of my life.

WILLIAM J. GAITHER

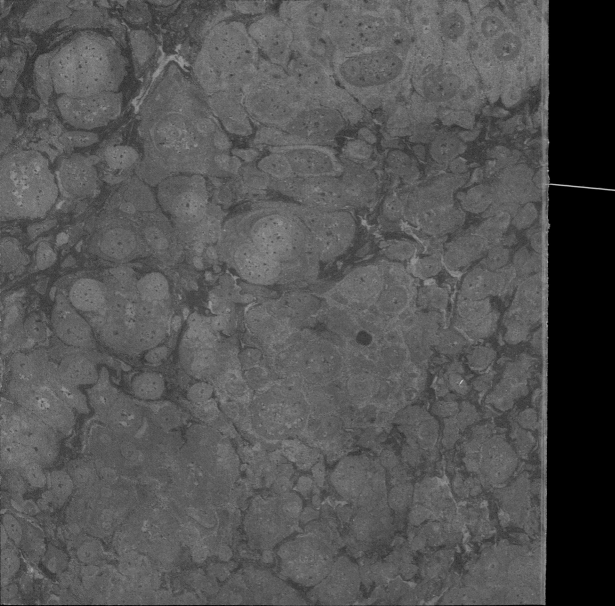